What is it like now...?

At home

Heinemann
LIBRARY

Schools Library and Infomation Services

Tony Pickford

www.heinemann.co.uk/library
Visit our website to find out more information about Heinemann Library books.

To order:
 Phone 44 (0) 1865 888066
 Send a fax to 44 (0) 1865 314091
Visit the Heinemann Bookshop at www.heinemann.co.uk/library to browse our catalogue
and order online.

First published in Great Britain by Heinemann Library, Halley Court, Jordan Hill, Oxford OX2 8EJ,
a division of Reed Educational and Professional Publishing Ltd. Heinemann is a registered trademark
of Reed Educational & Professional Publishing Ltd.

OXFORD MELBOURNE AUCKLAND JOHANNESBURG BLANTYRE
GABORONE IBADAN PORTSMOUTH (NH) USA CHICAGO

Designed by Celia Floyd
Illustrations by Jo Brooker
Originated by Dot Gradations
Printed in Hong Kong/China

ISBN 0431 15000 1   (hardback)
07 06 05 04 03
10 9 8 7 6 5 4 3 2

ISBN 0431 15006 0   (paperback)
07 06 05 04 03
10 9 8 7 6 5 4 3 2 1

British Library Cataloguing in Publication Data
Pickford, Tony
    What is it like at home?
    1. Home – Juvenile literature
    I. Title
    640

Acknowledgements
The Publishers would like to thank the following for permission to reproduce photographs:
Collections: Graham Burns p7, John Callan p9, Liz Stares p23; Eye Ubiquitous: Paul Seheult pp5, 14,
Paul Thompson pp25, 27; J Allan Cash: p21; John Birdsall Photography: pp6, 16, 17; Sally and Richard
Greenhill: pp11, 12, 15; Sylvia Cordaiy Photo Library: Geoffrey Taunton p22, J Worker p24; Tografox:
Bob Battersby pp10, 26, 29; Travel Ink: David Toase p28; Trevor Clifford: p4; Tudor Photography: p20.

Cover photograph reproduced with permission of John Birdsall.

Contents

What are homes? 4

Different types of homes 6

My address 8

Inside every home 10

My room 12

Our home 14

The kitchen 16

A plan of a house 18

Building houses 20

Old and new homes 22

What are homes made of? 24

Outside your home 26

Activities 28

Find out for yourself 30

Glossary 31

Index 32

Words printed in **bold letters like these** are explained in the Glossary.

What are homes?

Homes are places where people live. A home might be a house on a busy street or a **bungalow** in a quiet, country lane. It might be a flat or apartment in a tall **tower block** in a city.

Some homes are large and some are small. Some homes have lots of land around them while others have none.

A home might be part of a building like this tower block.

Some people live in mobile homes.

Some homes might have lots of people living together. Others might be for just one person or a couple of people. Some people like to live in homes which they can move around, such as **caravans** or mobile homes.

In this book you will find out about different kinds of homes and also the things that you will find in many homes.

Different types of homes

What kind of home do you live in? Is your home a house that has land all around it? It might be a large amount of land or just a small garden.

Sometimes a row of houses is joined together. This is called a **terrace**. Streets of terraced houses are often found in towns and cities. You can also find terraced houses in the countryside.

This is a street of terraced houses in a large town.

*Sometimes old buildings, which were once **factories** or **warehouses**, are made into flats where many people can live.*

A house which stands on its own is called a **detached** house. Two houses joined together are **semi-detached**. A house with all its rooms on one floor is called a **bungalow**.

In towns and cities, some buildings can have many homes inside. These homes, called flats or apartments, are built side-by-side and on top of each other.

My address

Whatever type of home you live in you will have an address which tells everyone where you live. You can tell your friends and family your address so that they can send you letters and parcels. You should also know your address so that you can tell a police officer if you ever get lost.

A house in a street in a town will have an address like this:

16 Park Street,	*This is the number of the house and the name of the street.*
Whitley,	*This is the name of the town.*
Cheshire	*This is the county – a large area with lots of towns and villages inside it.*
CW2 3AZ	*These letters and numbers help the Post Office to sort letters and find your home. They are called a postcode.*

A house in the country might have an address like this:

Ivy Cottage,	*This is the name of the house. Sometimes there might also be a number.*
Abbey Lane,	*This is the road next to the house.*
Smallton,	*This is the name of the village.*
Near Whitley,	*This is the name of the nearest town.*
Cheshire	*This is the county.*
CW4 5PQ	*This is the postcode.*

All the letters and parcels that come to your home have your address on them.

Inside every home

Whatever their type, size or age, all homes have some similar things. All homes have a front door. The door might be on a **landing** of a block of flats or it might lead to a garden or the street. The front door is where visitors come to your home. How do you know when visitors are at your front door?

These front doors belong to **terraced** *houses.*

Most homes have at least one kitchen, bedroom, toilet and a place to have a shower or bath. The kitchen is often the busiest room in the home. This is where people cook their food and, sometimes, eat it too. A bedroom is important so that people can get a good night's sleep.

Sometimes the toilet is in a small room on its own or it might be in the same room as the bath or shower.

As well as having baths or showers, you might use a bathroom when you brush your teeth.

My room

Do you have a special room in your home? It might be a bedroom that you have all to yourself or it might be a room that you share with your brothers and sisters.

What sorts of things do you have in your room? You will probably have a bed. Bunk beds are good because they save space and leave room for things, such as desks or cupboards.

Different parts of your room will be used for different things – for sleeping, for storing things and for playing.

Try to make a plan of your room. The plan shows where everything is and what different parts of the room are used for. It is a **bird's eye view**.

A good way of making a plan is to make a model using building blocks. You can then look down on the model from above and draw what you see.

A plan of your bedroom might look something like this.

Our home

There are different kinds of homes. The picture below is of a **semi-detached** house in a town. A mum and dad and two children live there. Outside there is a small garden and a drive where the family parks their car.

There are lots of houses in the street with many families living close by. The children have friends to play with.

This family lives in a town. Their house is semi-detached.

This family lives on a farm in the countryside.

The house in this picture is on a farm in the countryside. A mum and dad and two children live here too. Outside the house there is a busy farmyard with a place to milk cows and a barn for the tractor.

The children can play in the fields around the farm. Most of the time they play on their own because their friends live far away. What is your home like? Do you have friends to play with?

The kitchen

The kitchen is an important room. It may have a refrigerator to keep food cool and a cooker. The cooker may have a **hob** for cooking food in pans and an oven for baking and roasting.

Many kitchens will also have another oven called a microwave for cooking food very quickly. In some homes the microwave is the only oven that is used.

It is good fun to help in the kitchen when food is being cooked.

After we have eaten our food, another job done in the kitchen is washing the dishes.

There will also be cupboards for storing food in bags, cans and packets. Food is usually bought at a supermarket or shop, but if you look closely at labels, you will see that the food that we eat comes from all over the world.

Many kitchens also have a washing machine for cleaning clothes. Kitchens have many machines for doing jobs that had to be done by hand in the past.

A plan of a house

This is a plan of a house that shows the rooms on the two floors. It is a plan made by a company which builds and sells new houses. Even before the houses are built, the people who sell the houses can show buyers how the rooms will be laid out.

first floor

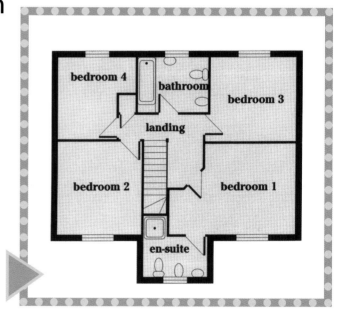

People might see plans like this if they are buying a new house.

ground floor

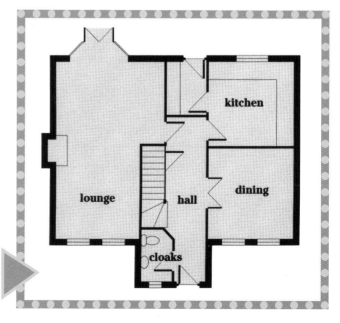

You could try to make a plan of your home in the same way that you made a plan of your room. Build a model of your house using building blocks and then look down on it to get a **bird's eye view**.

first floor

A plan of your house might look something like this.

ground floor

Building houses

A **building site** is where new homes are built and is a very dangerous place. You should never go there to play.

If your family is looking for a new home then you might visit a place like this. Some houses will have only the first few layers of bricks in place. These are called the foundations. There will be **scaffolding** around the houses so that workers can lay the bricks.

Workers have nearly finished building this house.

Some houses will be nearly finished. The walls will be in place but there might not be any **frames** or glass in the windows. Other houses will have windows and doors, but workers will be putting in kitchen units and electric wires.

Building sites are interesting places, but you must never go near one when you are on your own. They are dangerous places.

⚠ **Danger**
❗ **Keep out**

Old and new homes

In any area you will see homes of different kinds that have been built at different times. In towns and cities, some homes were built many years ago. The houses are often very close together. More **modern** homes in towns are usually built with gardens and places for cars to be parked.

*These **terraced** homes were built about 100 years ago for workers in the town.*

The homes in the picture below were also built 100 years ago. They have gardens and the area has wider roads and trees. They were built for workers, but not near the middle of the town. They are more like homes in the countryside.

Homes in or near the countryside often have more space around them. Sometimes modern homes are built to look old. Why do you think this is?

Port Sunlight is called a garden village because every house has a small garden.

What are homes made of?

How can you tell whether a home is old or new? One way is to look at the **materials** that have been used to build it. In the picture below, instead of brick or stone, wood has been used to build the house. Long pieces of wood have been put together to make a strong **frame**.

This very old house has a wooden frame. The pieces of wood make shapes and patterns.

This picture shows a pattern of bricks in a wall. Can you find different brick patterns in the walls of different houses?

Brick is a very common building material. When a bricklayer builds a wall he puts the bricks down in a pattern so that the wall is strong.

He will lay different bricks so that either the long side of the brick (called the stretcher) or the short side (the header) is facing out. The pattern the bricklayer uses is called a bond.

Outside your home

What is outside your home? A flat in a **tower block** in a city may have a **balcony** outside where people can sit on sunny days. There may be plants and flowers growing in pots and tubs. A home in a town might not have a garden, but children can go to a nearby park to play.

People living in this flat in a town have made a garden on the balcony.

Houses like this on the edge of a town usually have gardens around them.

On the edge of the town, houses may have gardens and a place to park a car. In the country, there may be lots of land around. Homes might have big gardens. There might also be a field nearby. Some fields might be used to grow plants and others may have animals in them, such as cows or sheep.

Activities

- An estate agent sells both new and older homes. Look in the window of an Estate Agent's shop and you will see cards which show the homes that are on sale. Can you make an Estate Agent's card for your home?

An estate agent helps people to sell their homes. The window is full of pictures of different houses and flats.

- If you look at the labels on packets and cans in the cupboards in your kitchen you will find that many of the foods come from very distant places. See if you can find these places on a globe or a map of the world in your school.

The food we eat comes from many different countries.

- You could use books in the library to find out about homes in other countries. If you have been to another country on holiday, think about how the homes there were different from your home.

Find out for yourself

Places to visit

To see homes that were built many years ago for workers in a factory, you could visit:

- Styal Village
  Wilmslow SK9 4LA

- New Lanark Mills
  Lanark ML11 9DB

Websites

Go to www.multimap.com and type in your postcode. You will soon see a map of the local area with your home in the centre.

Books

Linkers: Homes discovered through Geography, Karen Bryant-Mole, A & C Black, 2001

What was it like in the past? At home, Mandy Ross, Heinemann Library, 2002

Glossary

balcony a piece of floor with a rail around it outside an upstairs window

bird's eye view a view of a home from above

building site a place where new homes are being built

bungalow a house without any upstairs rooms

caravan a home with wheels that can be moved from place to place. Some people live in caravans, others use them just for holidays.

detached a house which is not attached to any other

factories big buildings where things are made using machines

frame material around the edge of something which gives it a shape

hob hot plates or rings for cooking food in pans

landing an area at the top of the stairs

materials what something is made of, such as bricks or cement

modern up-to-date

scaffolding a metal and wood frame used by a bricklayer

semi-detached two houses which are joined together

terrace a row of houses which are joined together

tower block a tall block of flats often found in a town or city

warehouses large buildings where things made in factories are stored before they are sold

Index

address 8, 9
bedroom 11, 12
bricks 20, 24, 25
building site 20
bungalow 4, 7
caravan 5
detached house 7
estate agents 28
factory 7
farm 15
flat 7, 10
front door 10
garden 6, 10, 14, 15, 22, 23, 27
kitchen 11, 16, 17
plan 13, 18, 19, 27
semi-detached house 7, 14
terraced house 6, 22
toilet 11
tower block 4, 26
warehouse 7
window 21